The Wild World of Animals

Baboons

Life in the Troop

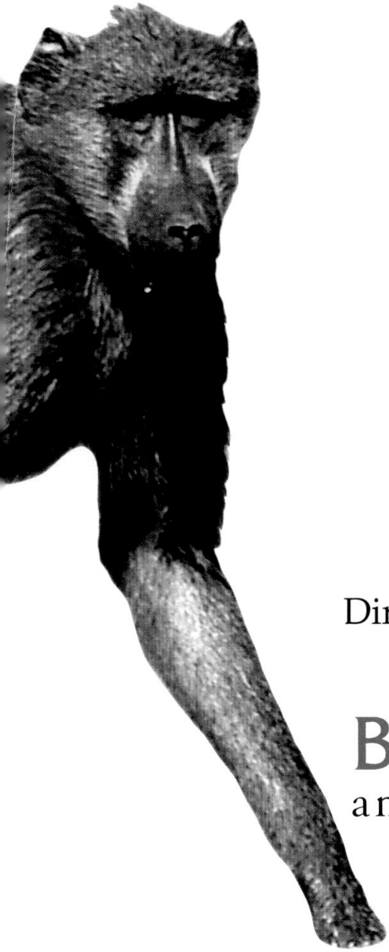

by Adele D. Richardson

Consultant:
Anne Warner
Director of Conservation and Education
The Oakland Zoo

Bridgestone Books
an imprint of Capstone Press
Mankato, Minnesota

Bridgestone Books are published by Capstone Press
151 Good Counsel Drive, P.O. Box 669, Mankato, Minnesota 56002
http://www.capstone-press.com

Library of Congress Cataloging-in-Publication Data
Richardson, Adele, 1966–
    Baboons: life in the troop/ by Adele D. Richardson.
    p. cm.—(The wild world of animals)
    Includes bibliographical references (p.24) and index.
    ISBN 0-7368-0961-9
    1. Baboons—Juvenile literature. [1. Baboons.] I. Title. II. Series.
QL737.P93 R55 2002
599.8′65—dc21   00-012512

Summary: An introduction to baboons describing their physical characteristics, habitat, young,
    food, predators, and relationship to people.

Editorial Credits

Erika Mikkelson, editor; Karen Risch, product planning editor; Linda Clavel, cover designer
    and illustrator; Heidi Schoof, photo researcher

Photo Credits

James P. Rowan, 4
Joe McDonald/Pictor, 6
John Shaw/TOM STACK & ASSOCIATES, 10
Michael Turco, 14
Root Resources, 1
Tom & Pat Leeson, cover, 8, 16
Visuals Unlimited/Joe McDonald, 12; Barbara Gerlach, 18; D. Long, 20

1 2 3 4 5 6 07 06 05 04 03 02

Table of Contents

Baboons 5

Baboons Are Mammals. 7

A Baboon's Habitat 9

What Do Baboons Eat? 11

Opposable Thumbs. 13

Mating and Birth. 15

Baboon Infants. 17

Protection from Predators. 19

Baboons and People 21

Hands On: Baboon Thumbs. 22

Words to Know 23

Read More 24

Internet Sites 24

Index. 24

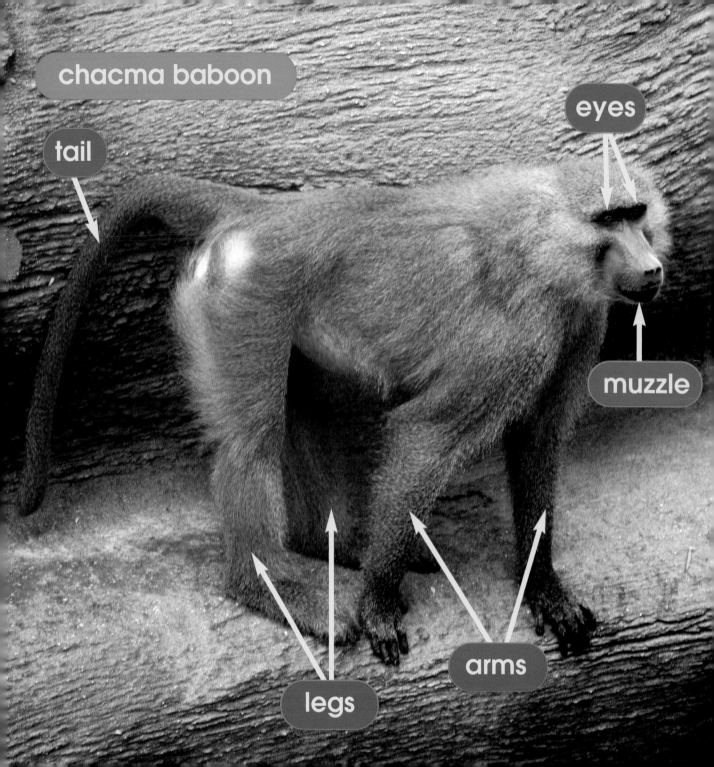

chacma baboon

tail

eyes

muzzle

legs

arms

Baboons

Baboons are large monkeys. Baboons have long muzzles. They have large, fang-like canine teeth. Baboons have long tails. Baboons walk on their long legs and arms.

muzzle
an animal's nose, mouth, and jaws

olive baboons

Baboons Are Mammals

Baboons are mammals. Mammals are warm-blooded animals with a backbone. Female mammals feed milk to their young. Most mammals are covered with hair or fur. Baboons have black, brown, red-brown, or yellow-brown fur.

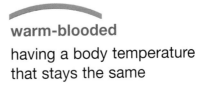

warm-blooded
having a body temperature
that stays the same

olive baboons

A Baboon's Habitat

Baboons live in Africa and on the Arabian Peninsula. Baboons' habitats are rocky areas and open grasslands. Baboons spend most of their time on the ground. Some baboons sleep in trees.

habitat
the place where an animal lives

FUN FACTS

The hamadryas baboon is one kind of baboon that lives on the Arabian Peninsula. Saudi Arabia is the largest country on this peninsula.

hamadryas baboon

What Do Baboons Eat?

Baboons eat many kinds of food. Grass is the most important food for baboons. They also eat fruit, leaves, and insects. Baboons sometimes kill and eat small animals.

olive baboon

Opposable Thumbs

Baboons have opposable thumbs. They can move their thumbs to meet their fingers. People use their thumbs in the same way. A baboon's foot works like its hand. A baboon can easily grasp objects with its hands and feet.

opposable
able to place something against something else; a thumb and a finger are opposable.

chacma baboons

FUN FACTS !

A baboon troop can have 4 to 750 baboons. Members of a troop groom each other every day. They use their fingers to pick out dirt, insects, and dry skin.

Mating and Birth

Baboons live together in groups called troops. Males fight each other to become the troop's leader. Female baboons then mate with the leader. Young baboons are born about six months later.

olive baboon and infant

Baboon Infants

Young baboons are called infants. Baboon infants are born at night. They have dark, soft fur and pink skin. Infant baboons' fur changes color when they are 3 to 6 months old. Infants stay close to their parents for at least one year.

olive baboon

FUN FACTS !

Baboons use
loud, barking
calls to warn
other baboons
that a predator
is near.

Protection from Predators

Male baboons help protect the troop from predators. Leopards, lions, and cheetahs hunt and eat baboons. Male baboons fight together to scare away predators. They scratch and hit with their strong arms. Baboons also bite with their large, canine teeth.

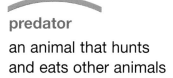

predator
an animal that hunts
and eats other animals

gelada baboons

Baboons and People

People can help baboons by not destroying baboons' habitats. People build houses and farm on land where baboons live. Some people set up parks and reserves for the baboons. Baboons have space to live and food to eat in these protected areas.

Hands On: Baboon Thumbs

Opposable thumbs help baboons climb trees and grasp objects. These thumbs also help baboons eat.

What You Need

A leaf
A banana or orange
A pebble
Masking tape

What You Do

1. Lay the leaf, fruit, and pebble on a table. Imagine the objects are foods a baboon would eat. The pebble could be an insect.
2. Use masking tape to tape your thumb to the palm of your hand. Try to pick up each object without using your thumbs. Try to peel the fruit.
3. Next, try to pick up the objects using your thumbs. Try to peel the fruit.

Using your thumb and fingers makes it easier to grasp objects. This also is true for the baboon. A baboon's opposable thumbs help it pick up and eat food. Baboons can survive in the wild because of their opposable thumbs.

Words to Know

grassland (GRASS-land)—a large open area of grass

infant (IN-fuhnt)—a young baboon

mammal (MAM-uhl)—a warm-blooded animal that has a backbone; female mammals feed milk to their young.

mate (MATE)—to join together to produce young; male and female baboons mate to produce infants.

peninsula (puh-NIN-suh-luh)—an area of land surrounded by water on three sides; some baboons live on the Arabian Peninsula northeast of Africa.

troop (TROOP)—a group of baboons

warm-blooded (warm-BLUHD-id)—having a body temperature that stays the same

Read More

Holmes, Kevin J. *Baboons.* Animals. Mankato, Minn.: Bridgestone Books, 2000.

Woods, Mae. *Baboons.* Checkerboard Animal Library. Edina, Minn.: Abdo & Daughters, 1998.

Internet Sites

Baboons
http://sailfish.exis.net/~spook/bab.html
The Oakland Zoo: Hamadryas Baboon
http://www.oaklandzoo.org/atoz/azbaboon.html
Sierra Safari Zoo—Baboons
http://www.sierrasafarizoo.com/animals/baboons.htm

Index

Africa, 9
Arabian Peninsula, 9
fruit, 11
fur, 7, 17
grass, 11
grasslands, 9
habitats, 9, 21
infants, 17
mammals, 7

monkeys, 5
muzzles, 5
opposable thumbs, 13
predators, 19
reserves, 21
tails, 5
teeth, 5, 19
trees, 9
troop, 15, 19